Art Now   Rudolf Hoflehner

Rudolf Hoflehner

WERNER HOFMANN

85 MONOCHROME PLATES

T & H

THAMES AND HUDSON LONDON

As a rule, every artist thinks his latest work his best. To agree with this is not always easy for someone who is trying to expound on an artist's work, for he has already built up his own image of the artist and does not want to see the outlines being blurred and the balance disturbed. It does not matter whether the "last" work (soon to be followed by others) strikes him as significant and necessary, or something quite puzzling and alien which will not fit in with the previous pattern. The critic has his own idea about the artist, and he will not willingly surrender it. Also—though he takes care to keep this to himself—he is convinced that he knows in which direction the artist should develop. That alone makes him a prejudiced observer. And he may even profess to gaze with admiration at the artist, while all the time his gaze is more critical than admiring.

One should distinguish here between two attitudes. On the one hand there is the law of organic growth: the artist does what he does because he must. He is a slave of those compulsive forces which were latent in him from the very beginning, and the critic's task is to lay them bare. Intellectual economy is dear to such critics. Interpretations that they have already established (and already published) are not to be discarded but co-ordinated with what is new. Cracks and fissures can be smoothed over with a little rhetorical putty. Usually, if convinced of organic development, one seizes a magic wand which enables one to hear the grass grow and meanings talk aloud. What is now plainly to be seen growing above ground was always there in the seed; there is no deviation from the past. One can simply equate x with y, and then with z.

This attitude leads to the formulation of a norm. Deviations may be suffered in silence, but they are pushed aside as of no consequence. The only important thing is what fits in to this concept. The critic seizes on the past to impose conformity to the norm. One should not hold it against him, nevertheless—but if only he would admit it! He alone charts the mainstream of development. He suppresses whatever does not fit into his picture in favour of factors that will add up to some harmonious whole.

Opposed to the smooth, standardizing outlook, which attempts to apply to the arts the adage "natura non facit saltus", is one which grants genius the privilege of taking unpredictable decisions, to behave as oddly and capriciously as it pleases, and again and again to throw everything (including its own achievements) over the windmill. The current "dernier cri" is quite without precedent; it is an advance into the Future, the Unknown, which nobody can sidetrack. Anyone using this formula has managed to get rid of all the ballast of organic development. According to this formula the artist is not only always questioning himself but is continually annihilating whatever he has previously done. Before he can give birth to his new creation, he must wipe the slate clean, he must achieve absolute freedom in which to work by breaking away from the bonds of precedent. One can see how the criteria of originality and spontaneity— which play such a large rôle in "modern" artistic judgments—lead to accepting every "true" work of art presented to us as an isolated value in a void where no comparisons are valid. Thus whereas genetical analysis, mindful of the demands of continuity, postulates a basic pattern or *leitmotiv*, this point of view is aware of the danger of the cliché and the stencil.

In actual fact an artist's activity, whether intellectual or material, is the outcome of a war waged between the forces of continuity and discontinuity. Were it merely the result of a development following organic rules, it would not be intriguing enough to hold the attention of a spectator who knew the "pattern". If it were a punctuated succession of unrelated and unique creations the thread of continuity would be lacking to hold his attention. What actually occurs in a work of art is an endless dialectical process in which bridges are built and then burnt; the past is summoned and in the same breath dismissed; tradition is evoked and destroyed. The critic who wants to follow this creative contest is faced with a real dilemma. For isn't his endeavour to stress continuity just as legitimate as his search for what is new and now apparent for the first time?

That must be said, for the critic not only has the right, but also the duty, to reveal what he knows of his own standpoint. The more he writes about an artist the more acutely he is faced with the difficulties of his *métier*. Two years ago, when I was writing the text for a catalogue of Hoflehner's work, I began with the following characterization: "The first impression is: piercing, thrusting, firmly entrenched, striving forces. Energy, sharp as a knife and wounding. Armoured images of defence and aggression. Hard breaks, abrupt turns. Clubs, joints, levers, rods. Taut verticals piled up in splints or stretched like elastic: no transition from limb to limb, no flowing contour, only a dissonant sticking of fragments together. No shapes to feel at home with, but ones that bid you keep your distance."

No sooner had this summing up been written than it was shown to be biassed by wishful thinking — I was guilty of taking a part for the whole. It was dependent on one particular group of works which, even then in the winter of 1963, was already a closed chapter. As far as the *Doric Figure* of 1958 (*Ill.* 9) or the *Stoic Figure* of 1959 (*Ill.* 19) are concerned the description fits absolutely, but applied to later work it is only partially true.

Indeed such a characterization shows up both the advantages and disadvantages of simplification. True, it deals with first-class examples that even today I would rate among the most powerful and monumental of Hoflehner's works, but I neglected to point out what was unique to this group of sculptures, and unrepeatable. If today I ask myself which of all Hoflehner's works are the most challenging I would not hesitate to nominate those inspired by Greece (*Ills.* 9, 10, 18, 19, 20, 21). Let us, therefore, begin with these.

Faced with something new in art, people immediately react in one of two fundamentally different ways. Even before they say "that makes sense", or "it's nonsense", they have to consider the material aspect of the work in front of them. They may approach it with reverence or bewilderment. They are already prejudiced. Whoever believes himself capable of doing what the artist has "shown" him is also quite out of touch, and his answer to the "sense or nonsense" question is wide of the mark.

In this respect a sculptor working in iron, like Hoflehner, has one initial advantage over his detractor. Whatever sins he may be accused of, lack of effort is not one of them. Looking at his over life-sized figures, such as *Sisyphus* (*Ill.* 18), the first impression is of the concentrated physical energy needed to create them. They demonstrate a power, as proud as it is uninhibited, which is achieved by exploiting to the full the

The Studio in Praterstern, Vienna

physical property of the raw material with all its weight and solidity. Here one can see before one's very eyes how the articulated elements are piled up, one on top of the other. Spherical and square blocks, knobs and segments of circles are added layer by layer and so welded together that there is no illusion of an unbroken continuity. The uncompromisingly exhibited planes and edges are born of the desire for a violent, fragmented form. This is formed by the cutting blow-lamp before whose tremendous cleaving power the raw material shrinks and surrenders up its apparent impenetrability. Dramatic furrows bear witness to the attack of the technical process. One can see that this action is rooted in destruction: the material which was originally planned for other uses must first of all be taken away and alienated from its original sphere of utility. Awkward fragments are cut from polished units that have been produced with mechanical precision. Taken by themselves they are meaningless bits of work, without even those associative dimensions inherent in the shape of a leaf or a pebble. But it is precisely this that makes them usable.

First comes the preparatory formation of the letters, and then follows the building of words that is the real modelling, the layering, the clamping together and intertwining of the various parts. The obviously exposed method of work guides the reaction of the spectator looking at the completed work. At first the image of injury and damage is bound up with the various phases of preparing the material, but this presently changes to speculation on the threatening and aggressive energy of the sculpture. The rugged act of violence which called these figures into being now lives on in them with a piercing sharpness which is employed against the spectator who accepts their challenge.

Whence comes this process that so plainly stresses the fragmentation of its products, that never finishes a rounded-off whole but offers crippled gestures in which the question mark of the unfinished and the inconsistent is inherent? Put like this, the question of how the form comes into being already touches upon the sphere of significance. Indeed it is a question that can no longer be ignored: we can no longer talk of the arrangement of form without considering the emotion it calls forth in us. In his evocations of the Greek world Hoflehner used the technique of montage. The initial units which he uses are built up from anonymous *objets trouvés*, not those picked up from a rubbish heap but those which occur *en masse* in iron foundries. This fact suggests that one should take a look at Hoflehner's connections with Cubism (montage) and Surrealism (*objets trouvés*). But to do that we must first look further back into the past.

The artistic world which was founded on the Renaissance set itself the task of subduing the perceptible world to a rational aspect. It created an ideal of oneness and continuity in the relationship between figures and space found in the external world. To realize this concept the disciplines of central perspective and anatomy were brought into play. If space had previously been a shrine for, and a symbol of, something quite remote, with no possible connection with our own contemporary existence, now an empirical bond of intimacy links together the picture and the spectator, who finds himself a participant in the painted scene. Perspective subordinated every component of the picture to the rule of the whole composition; the unbroken space continuum joined together foreground and background. With the illusion of depth there is at the

The Studio in Krieau, Vienna

same time a heightening of realism in the details that go to build up the picture—men and beasts, trees and chattels attain a more intense physical individuality; that is that autocracy and self-assurance of corporeal appearance whose deployment is called for on the stage of the three-dimensional picture.

The depth of the picture balances the bodily homogeneity which makes every detail of the picture a compact entity. In other words the human figure is no longer—as in early medieval or Byzantine miniatures—a mixed composition built up of heterogeneous parts, but a homogeneous creation, the artistic expression of an indivisible and organic whole. Then, as a logical consequence, follows a further step in regard to the material aspect of the picture, for the homogeneous surface offsets the formal space continuity. The medieval picture exhibits a varied surface and breaks up into essentially different planes: painting is mixed with areas of ornamentally embossed gold work, or may be interrupted by having precious stones inset. In the Renaissance there is one single surface—and that is exclusively "painting", the whole of the extent being moulded by the painter's creative brush work.

All these premises were contradicted by the Cubists. In their painting objects surrender their organic unity and are segmented. In place of a continuous flow of space seen from one single viewpoint there is a welter of broken-up planes and axes. Finally the process of montage introduces collage, and the picture surface, up till now homogeneous, is broken up by the insertion of solid fragments of real objects (e. g. snippets of newspapers) and becomes again heterogeneous. The actual work of painting is consequently restricted and is not applied to the whole surface of the picture. Instead of painting the label on a bottle, the label itself is stuck on the picture. This means the surface is no longer homogeneous but, at least in part, incorporates disparate features.

Sculptural creation also lends itself to the possibilities of heterogeneity: a three-dimensional montage can be created from *objets trouvés*. Lipchitz has carried this process to its utmost limits. He exhibits sculpture which can be dissected into its initial elements. On the one hand the preliminary state of the finished product is demonstrated, and on the other hand the artist is shown to be the exponent and sovereign discoverer of an individual reality. On the whole, one of the most important and far-reaching achievements of Cubism is to prove that artistic apprehension of reality need not only copy reality but can also create it. Thus the artist is freed from the thrall of illusionism and is endowed with his own power and authority to use symbols. Potentially he is capable of anything. From now on he can make everything; more important, he can now create art from everything—even from pig iron.

If one explores Hoflehner's relationship to the achievements of Cubism one comes to the following conclusion: his method has given a dramatic and romantic twist to the principle of montage. The collision of heterogeneous masses is not harmonized as in classical Cubism, but dissonance is sought after and stressed. The technique of welding practised by the Constructivists of the "twenties and thirties", which refined everything to an immaculate functionalism, is brutalized and barbarized by Hoflehner. True, in his work he is acutely conscious of the present day and he uses the left-overs of this technical age, but he thrusts them back into an archaic ambience. In the *Doric*

Cutting

Figure (*III*. 9) he handles iron as though he were the first to master it, straightforwardly and powerfully, renouncing any artistic slickness.

Faced with such sculptures the question of how they function does not even arise, nor even the wish to dissect them. Therein lies their protest. The world for which one is here trying to find a symbol is the opposite of the constructional, functionally planned and factual world of the engineer. And just because of this the technical world is again and again conjured up as an antithesis. Its smooth comprehensibility is brought up against jagged impenetrability, its economical power faced with the wild and extravagant expansion of power that sweeps all before it, and its absolute utility faced with complete uselessness. Against the optimistic claim of the Constructivists to reconcile art and present-day reality, Hoflehner creates images that reject any intrusion of the technological world. Yet in these creations the technical world of production is conquered by its own means and in a dialectical sense "cancelled out". The man who shapes these sculptures is no romantic blacksmith content with his hammer and anvil, but an artist who works with the most modern technical apparatus. From which it follows that one can use the instruments and processes of the technical age and yet produce objects which have nothing to do with the most obvious tendencies of this age. The artist's answer to those principles of practicality and "the mediocrity" which are reducing our world more and more to the same level is the unrepeatable individuality of his work.

If one follows this up further one comes to that plane of symbols which has already been mentioned. Hoflehner brings to the creative principle of welding various pieces together a significance which had been left unrealized by the Cubists and had been actively opposed by the Constructivists who succeeded them. It became for him a metaphor of a world consisting only of individual entities. That is the sceptical answer to the Renaissance desire for a sensible, harmonious and coherent world—an answer which Cubism, with its obsession with form, evaded in as much as it (though completing the break with homogeneity and continuity) did not allow this process fully to ripen into tragic dimensions. It was exactly this dimension that Hoflehner sought in his "Grecian" figures, which thus existentially deepen the significance of the welded form. He once wrote in a letter: "The title *Sisyphus* is to be understood in an allusive sense as used by Camus ... and the 'condition humaine' is my symbol of life for an absurd hero of the irrational in the mechanical routine, who in spite of it responds to life and grows greater than his individual self."

Surrealism also came to terms with the thematics of the absurd. Here it became the cynical opposition to the Idealists—Mondrian and his circle—who proclaimed a world which could be bound down by an equation of geometrical form. But the equations of the Surrealists have no solution: there is always something puzzling and obscure left over which escapes any rational approach and laughs at vain attempts to pin it down. But the enduring importance of the Surrealists lies not only in showing optimistic Utopians the reverse side of the world, with which they hope quickly to be on terms, but to show a reverse that is out-and-out incommensurable. It also lies in their freeing the inventive activity of the artist from being formally held to account, and leading it

Polishing

into fresh and significant paths: to the land of poetry and magic, of dreams and idols. When Hoflehner says, "there is no clear, straightforward problem of form, but a spiritual attitude to the world which must be made manifest through form", he is expressing an axiom of the Surrealists. And he thereby gives notice that he will, with his creations, push on to spheres beyond the aesthetic: that form in itself has for him no importance but as a means to an end. This conviction is in conformity with his admiration of three artists whose work is strongly bound up with Surrealism: Brancusi, Giacometti and Gonzalez.

It would be a mistake to try to pin down exactly this connection with Surrealism and its conceptions. It leaves aside, for example, the sick humour, the irony of the *double entendre,* as well as comic understatement. The hard strain in Surrealist fantasy is quite alien to Hoflehner. He is also far too committed to the maximal straightforward meaning of his craft to be willing to exchange this for the possibility of interesting and startling combinations. And yet I would assert that the Surrealist factor, properly interpreted, is not only more primary but also more essential to Hoflehner's work than the expressively heroic Constructivism to which he surrendered in the late 'fifties. Would *Sisyphus* (*III*. 18), according to this, be looked on as a foreign body, or *Doric Figure* (*III*. 9) a wantonly imposed deviation from the "general line"? If so, then the special attention given here to this group of works must appear unjustified.

Nevertheless, the answer is that it was with the pathos of these sculptures that Hoflehner opened the way to a strong, monumental creative style. In creating these works he achieved a new range of means of communication, or rather, in these works he added to his humanistic and artistic desire for self-assertion signals of protest which were necessary to prove himself to himself and to the world. Because of this I believe that this group of works will always constitute one of the highlights of his creation, but a highlight which combines the compact punch of a manifesto with its surpassing pathos.

So it is understandable that this extreme evocation of tragic *Weltgefühl* came to an end, perhaps had to come to an end. Also, the universal acclaim given these particular works when they dominated the Biennale in Venice in 1960 may have partly helped to lower the tension. Now his mature creative self-confidence assumed another form. Since this had much in common with an earlier creative period (compare *III*. 40 with *III*. 2; *III*. 41 with *III*. 3) it should be discussed first.

When, in 1951, Hoflehner turned to iron, he himself was at first unaware of the monumental possibilities of the material. He had previously worked in wood, not by carving blocks but by using slender branches and supple osiers which he wove into creations of great lyrical charm. Often they bore some resemblance to fish-traps, and often to birds' nests, but always they were symbolical of growth, lyrically tender and pellucid, almost Asiatic in their significant restraint. No wonder then that at first iron was treated as a linear element, which could be bent and intertwined. Surprisingly rich spatial designs, which combined lightness with decorative charm, were the result. The handling of these imaginary scales called for careful orchestration. It branches out into space, but it is worth while to observe the effect in silhouette of the linear form. It is against a light background that these "cyphers" are most effective.

Wood Sculpture, 1950, 2 m (6 ft. 6 in.)

Wire Sculpture, 1952, 37 cm (14 ⁵/₈ in.)

Figuration, 1953, 22 cm (8 ⁵/₈ in.)

Gradually, in competition with the horizontal development, the verticals assert themselves, often in direct contact with Wotruba (*Ill.* 1). But with the vertical there arises a new problem. If heretofore the iron had to conform to a linear and skeletal conception of form, now new strains and structural needs necessitated a more solid body. The *Figuration* of 1953 (page XI) shows very prettily how the inventive fantasy, drawing back from its spreading ramifications, is firmly axial and screened off in space. The comparatively insignificant parenthetical inner figure stands in a space formed by boldly braced curves and bars (a mode of sculpture which we shall often meet again). In this figure an intellectual *leitmotiv* is already hinted at: the shrine, which encloses and protects.

In 1954 Hoflehner received a grant from UNESCO which enabled him to spend six months in Greece. The importance of this trip cannot be over-estimated. In the past one spoke of an educational tour and an educational experience. But nowadays things are different. An artist, coming to Greece in the middle of the twentieth century, can only turn his back on a civilization whose chief business is uninterruptedly to musealize itself and its past. For him the Mediterranean world, simplified by looking back at it from such a distance, has something primitive and straightforward, an intense vitality drawn in lapidary and sweeping outline which is a challenge to creative thought.

For Hoflehner that meant, by and large, the perception that beyond the formal possibilities of "transmutation", which until now had been almost his sole concern, there lay the challenge to endow a work of art with the magical, compulsive power of "evocation". The works of the following years aim at doing this (*Ills.* 3, 4, 5, 6). They deal with a fundamental human characteristic of consciously standing upright though often the motif is changed to that of striding forward. The dignity and vulnerability of human existence are here visually embodied. The modelling is treated like a sketch and does not hesitate to spurn anatomical convention and subordinate the whole body to the verticals of the legs—it is here we see the origin of the theme which was later taken up in "cleavage" and the split sculptures (*Ill.* 6). In addition to this, the hollowed-out inner space makes the symbolical function of the legs clearer, and the bar serves both to draw attention to and to protect the central space whose content remains unexplained. In *The Strider* (*Ill.* 5) of 1957 the correlation is already formulated which will later form the basis of a sexual symbolism: the spike, a Janus-headed bar tilted sideways, and the notched cleft which gapes between. Anatomically seen, these transverse curved bars of metal may have been inspired by shoulders or pelvis—an example of the alienating transposition of motifs.

But the concept of vulnerability is not always present in these figures, especially not in those where significant unity and finality reject every reminder of the 'condition humaine', that is, when they are remote from any animal dimension (*Ills.* 5, 6). Without appearing either harsh or repellent there is something in their outline which demands distance. They should be placed either on a high base or in a niche.

The artistic technique which endows them with this severe unapproachability and at the same time takes away their vulnerability is frontality. Just to stand there, inactive—that has always been the visible manifestation of the commanding dignity of a superior power. Man, to fulfill himself, needs action and strife; a god need only be calmly pre-

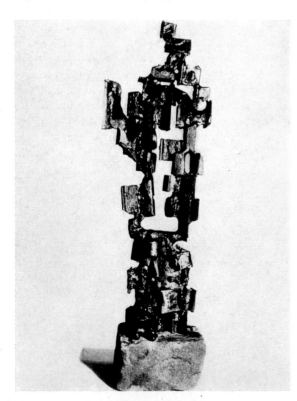

Figuration, 1953, 58 cm (22 $^7/_8$ in.)

sent. But what does action add? Expansion and space. And at what cost? The forfeiture of the formerly inviolate contour, the frictions and curtailments out of which the tortured form of the torso has been born (*Ills.* 7, 8). It should—indeed must—be walked round for every aspect of it is important and no one is predominant. Very different is the work of art which is designed to be seen frontally: here there is only one viewpoint, and even that is not left to the choice of the observer but is forced upon him. If you analyse a sculpture in the round, that can and should be seen from all sides, you have the privilege of free choice: if you accept the restraint of frontality you must surrender yourself to its spell and acquiesce in its limitations. Your pursuit of the work of art will lead to spheres beyond the aesthetic. Or rather an examination of the work for formal beauties will eventually turn into a confrontation with it which leads to a spiritual, and not merely an aesthetic, resolution.

Agon, 1958 (*III.* 13) is at the same time the apogee and the end of the tendency to frontalize. The idol-like intransigence of this armed prize-fighter has its humanistic counterpart in the *Split Figure* (*III.* 8). It is an end because already the treatment of form is paraphrasing itself. It is no longer naked and lapidary, but heavily ornamented. It stands there with a highly burnished finish; its axial symmetry is magnificent, polished and heraldic. But a certain superficiality can be sensed. One can predict the formula and the reactions which it will call forth. It is not surprising that Hoflehner, aware of this danger, immediately afterwards made a complete *volte face*, and began looking in the direction that was finally to lead to *Sisyphus* (*III.* 18) and *Condition Humaine* (*III.* 20). One can understand, looking at *Agon*, why the subsequent group of works call forth comments like "brutalization" and "barbarization".

Baudelaire, in his *Salon of 1846*, wrote a short chapter which sought to answer the question "Why is sculpture so boring?" The art of sculpture, it declares, belongs to the past because the possibilities of expression it offers cannot compete with those of painting. Already in Leonardo one can read something very similar. That is the outlook of an era whose aesthetic, based on illusionism, found its supreme values expressed in painting. And if one thinks of the mediocre exhibits in the Paris Salon which discredited the idea of sculpture, one can easily understand Baudelaire's contemptuous verdict.

A lot has altered since then. Nowadays we recognize that the revolution that has taken place in sculpture during our century is equal to that which has occurred in painting. Both critics and collectors have become sculpture-conscious. An eloquent example of this is the spontaneous public reaction to Hoflehner's appearance on the international scene at Venice in 1960, although they had neither been prepared for his work nor had their attention been drawn to it. Here was once more an artist who proved how acute Baudelaire's insight was when he said about sculpture although pejoratively that "its origin is lost in the mists of time". Today we see in this re-encounter with the elemental—Gauguin, Derain and Brancusi blazed the trail—a positive criterion and the warranty for an idiom which does not shun difficulties.

The dramatic eruption of the "Grecian" figures, which were acclaimed by the public as a "tour de force", might have been a temptation to repetition. But Hoflehner chose to follow a different path. For him the Biennale was a caesura, and his greatest gain from it was the determination not to cling to a successful formula. The works that immediately followed (*Ills.* 24, 25, 26, 27, 29, 30) at first give one a shock of surprise which is followed by the realization that these works hark back to distant beginnings and both radicalize and develop them. Basically this new vocabulary rests on two works of the early fifties (*Ills.* 2, 3). Their main characteristic is the employment in the central axis of a form jutting out towards the spectator, in one case a sloping wedge, in the other a sharp-edged curve. Many variations can spring from these fundamental motifs. The wedge may terminate in a sphere (*Ill.* 40) but this can also, when separated from the wedge, serve as a base for its swift escape (*Ill.* 31). And thence arise tangential contacts and bold feats of balance. The creations seem to spurn the ground or to wrench themselves free from it (*Ills.* 31, 32, 33, 34). In the background one can sense the ephemeral and vibrant elegance of the early spatial sketches.

But alongside these manneristic experiments are works which bring back the motifs to a central significance, the tension between two masses which are mutually interdependent: shell and kernel, wedge and fissure (*Ills.* 36, 37, 38, 39). Protective blocks, set upon firmly anchored legs, embrace the diagonal wedge, whose urgent power at the same time makes one question this embrace (it could also be interpreted as an injury). The wedge as an invader—is that not a meaning which unfairly attributes the original impetus to virile forces? Is it not, before it can procreate, itself one of the procreations of the female womb? If one looks at it from this point of view one is soon led back to archetypal relationships. One is reminded of the mythical conception of the indivisible coexistence of our first parents. Heinrich Zimmer, in his posthumously published book, *Myths and Symbols in Indian Art and Civilisation,* writes: "As the symbol of male creative energy, the lingam is frequently combined with the primary symbol of female creative energy, the yoni, the latter forming the base of the image with the former rising from its center. This serves as a representation of the creative union that procreates and sustains the life of the universe." But to point out such an interpretation should not deprive the "wedge" of its many meanings. The rampant form is not only identified with the phallus. If one compares it, for example, with a bird motif used to decorate an African temple (see page XIV) it is clear that its significance can be extended into the realms of vigilance, pre-eminence, dignity and power.

This tendency to create idols comes from an hermetic cast of mind. When selecting his forms Hoflehner is guided by his desire to find symbols that indicate concealment or exposure. A capsule, sphere, cave, shrine, hole or crevice are exposed to the percussive power of a wedge or rod, and always threatened by forcible entry or injury.

Another group is characterized by a massive breast work which is often tapered off like a bow (*Ill.* 55). One comes across this bowlike convexity already in the spike sculptures (see illustration), and it has perhaps some connection with the idols of the Cyclades whose heads are formed from a polished convex curve on which a vertical ridge rests for the nose. One can certainly connect the protective shield with the waning of the phallic motif. In *Male Figure III* (*Ill.* 48) just behind the hemispherical projection, a

Stake 1, 1960/61, 2.83 m (9 ft. 3 3/8 in.)

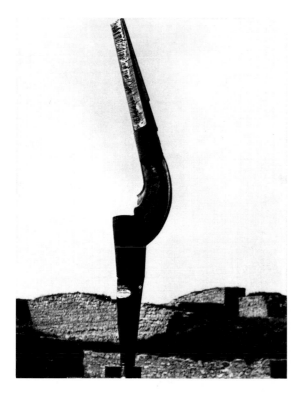

narrow intermediate space incites the hand to explore—a menace has become a fascination. It is precisely this that makes us in Rome put our hand into the "bocca della verità": this desire to play with the sinister, and with physical danger.

These works (*Ills.* 51, 52, 53, 54, 55) cut out the steep diagonal accent. Those sculptural energies, withdrawn from urgent linear extension, can now devote themselves without distraction to emphasizing and making tangible the central part of the body. Above all, this development leads to a clear demarcation of separate portions of the body. The verticals that ran through the whole sculpture now disappear and the legs become supports which display their true shape and seem to glory in their dignity. The formal diversity increases and with it the corporeal solidity and articulation. Also the change in technique is remarkable. The piecing together of dissonant parts is avoided and the additive element restrained. The surface treatment is more careful, the crusts and ridges are lost, and the expressive scratches and furrows of the blowlamp are used more sparingly. The burnishing machine polishes and gives anonymity to the material. This renunciation of "brutal" and "destructive" stimulants is appropriate to the hermetic character of the sculptures—it underlines their secretive sensibility, hinting at the arcane without dramatizing it.

It may be connected with this change that Hoflehner has begun more and more to work out his form designs in drawing. Earlier, the sketches were prosaic, precise notes on the work, but for a few years now they have revealed a representation of shapes, not based on a blocked-out dissonant arrangement, but on a linear interpenetration and a vibrating interweaving of dimensions. In the flat, his graphic sensitivity invents a new, organically-rounded corporality; when plastically transposed in space, this gives a new sensual flexibility to the possibilities of expression in iron. (See pages XVI–XXIII.)

When, in 1963, I wrote the piece about Hoflehner which I have already mentioned, the *Venus of Krieau* (*Ill.* 57) had not yet been created and I came to the following conclusion: "Whoever sees in art a means of affirming the absurd will recognize himself in these creations. Here he will find an artistic canon laid down for solitariness, which the increasing communalism of life demands. He will experience the power of resistance thus released and recognize that injury may have a meaning if transformed into endurance."

The later works make it necessary to correct this interpretation (*Ills.* 57, 59, 60 etc.). It is quite clear that now the symbol of the phallus is linked with that of the lap and pelvis. What, in the obviously female *Torso* of 1961 (*Ill.* 43), was shown as broken up fallowland is now instrumentated. The sphere, now freed from its fusion with the wedge (*Ill.* 40), is not only the sculptural epitome of fertile energy, it becomes the primeval cell from which all forms develop. The imaginative power is concentrated on the Great Mother, the Great Round. This evocation of fruitfulness has a triumphant undertone. Aggression, this painful escape from masculine hardness, is transformed into victorious expansion which knows no opposition: the conflicts between concealment and exposure give way before the process of growth which embraces them both. The work of sculpture becomes many-sided. The solid masses begin "to happen", X

Bird from Zimbabwe, Groote Schuur House, Capetown

but their dynamics continue in their orbits unforcedly, effortlessly and painlessly, spurred on by no existential necessity.

These metaphors of fruitfulness also hold a hint of the demands which the artist makes of his technique. They do not wish to borrow from the archetypal repertoire found in depth-psychology. It seems to me more probable that in his latest works Hoflehner is meditating on his calling, that he is taken up with the task of intuitively understanding the process of three-dimensional discovery of form—that is, how to invent emblems for the creative act of the sculptor of such a sort that the event and the form-growth are absolutely identical. Anyone who, in this comprehensive sense, pursues his revelation of self, knows himself to be in full mastery of his creative power. Should one interrupt him with a quick word of praise?

The Studio in Krieau, Vienna

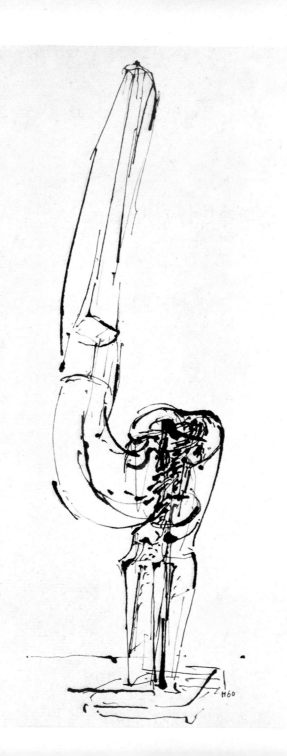

X

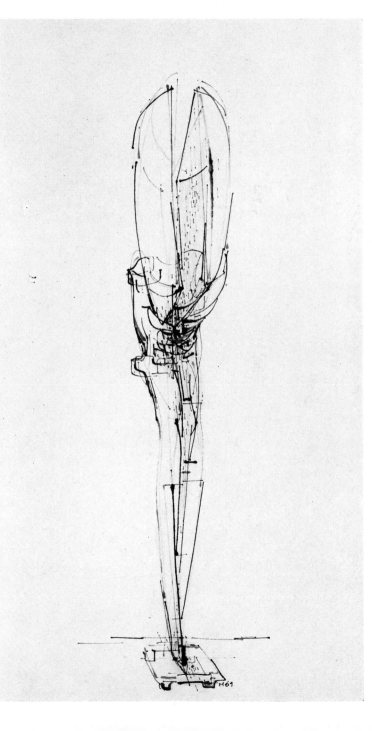

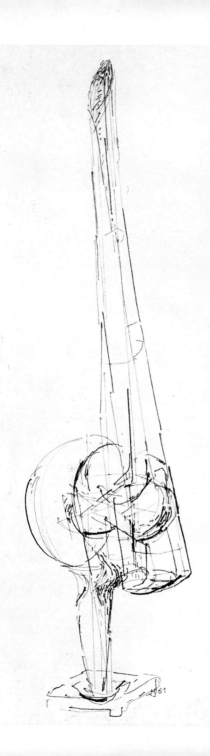

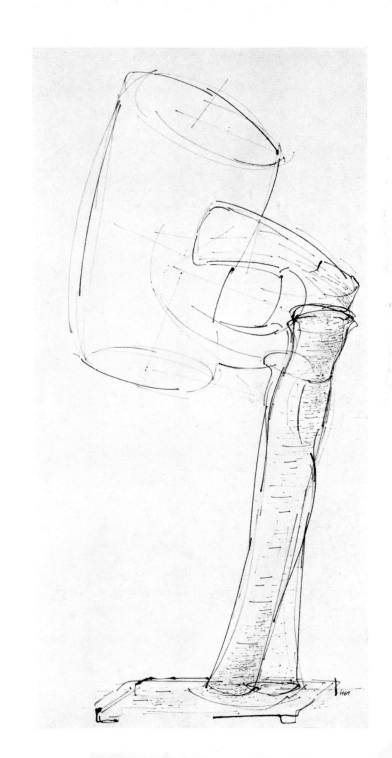

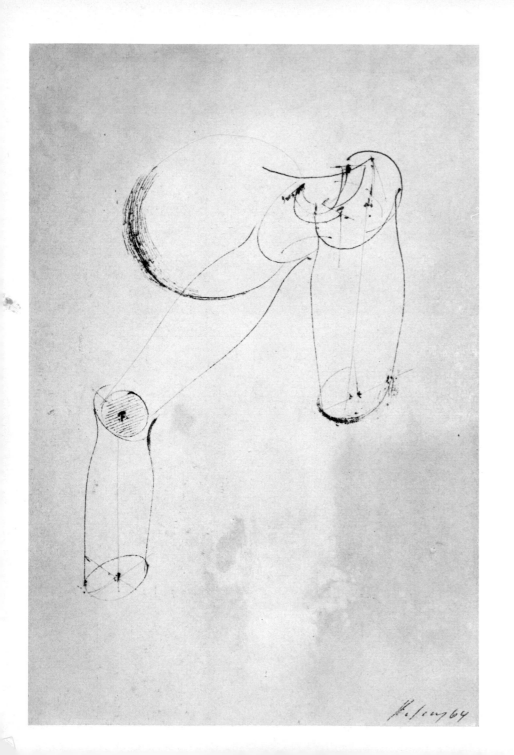

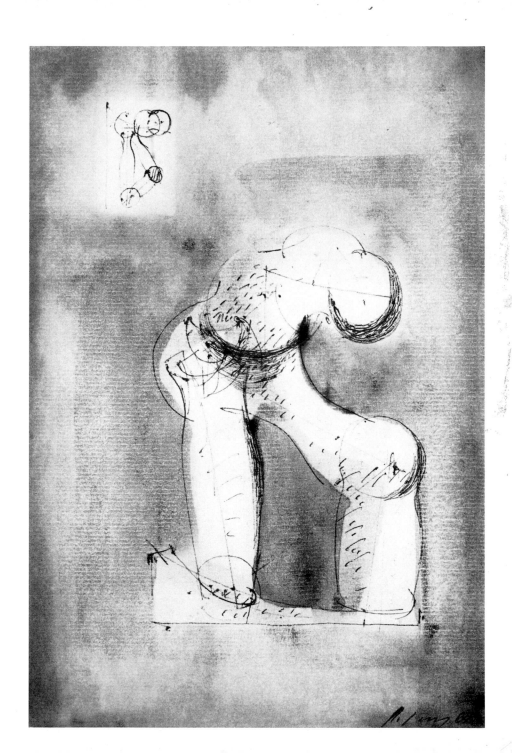

1

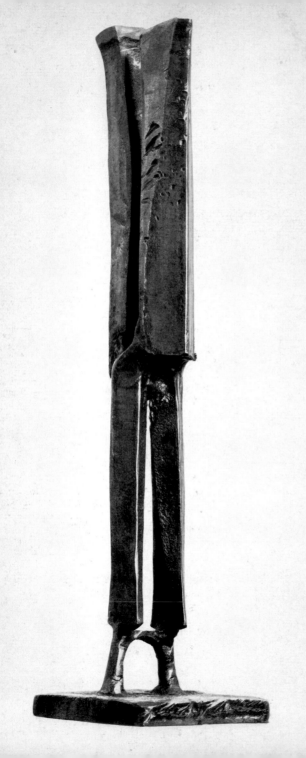

3

4

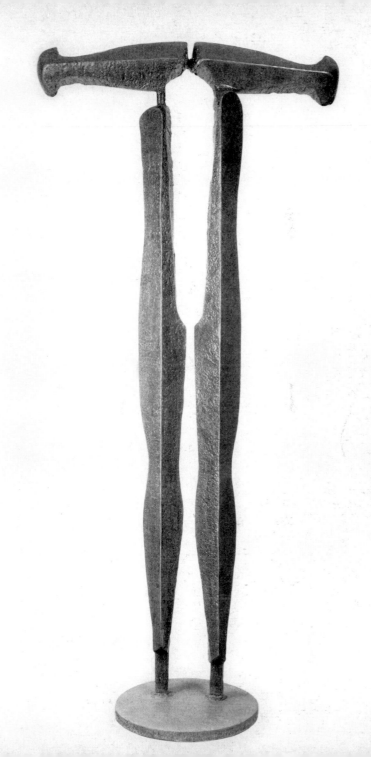

5

6

8

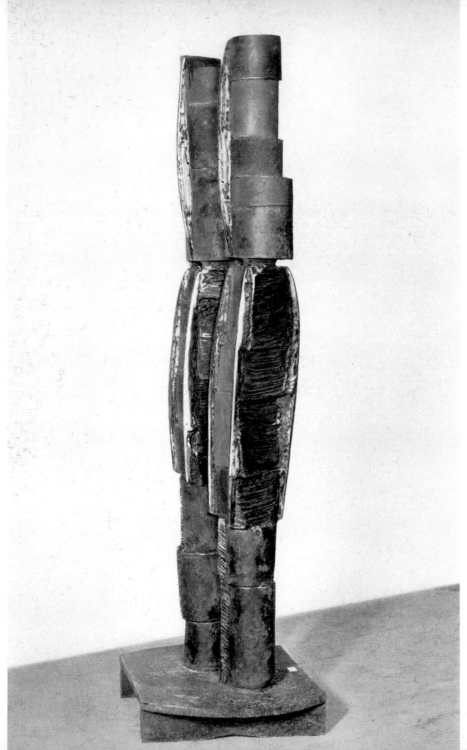

9

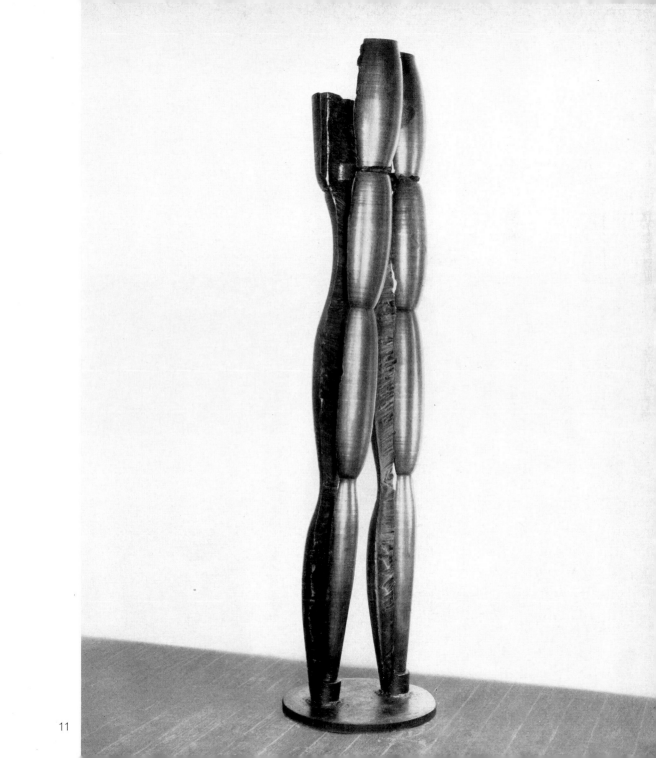

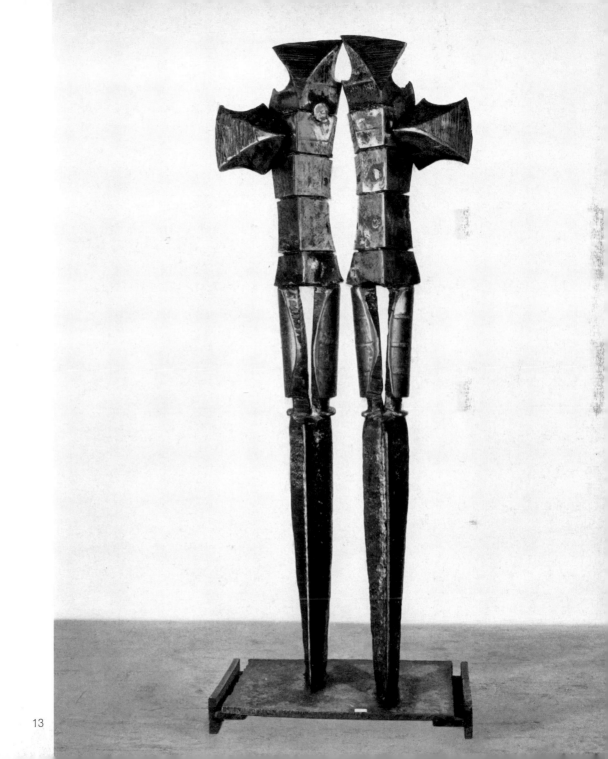

13

14

15

16

17

18

19

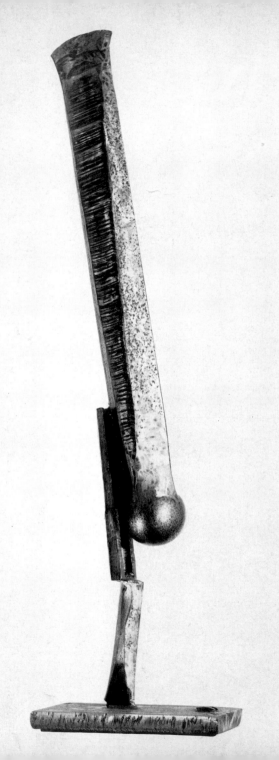

24

25

26

27

29

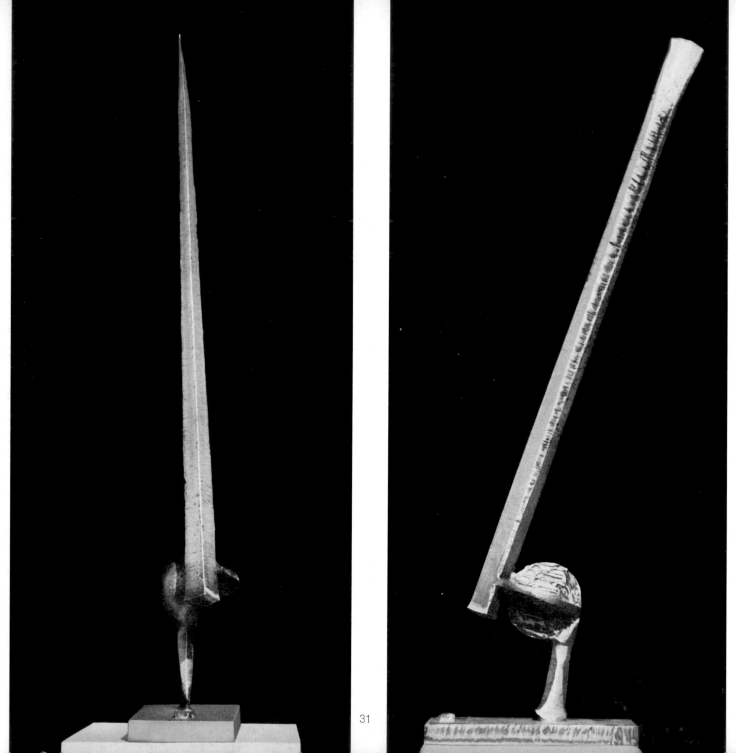

31

32

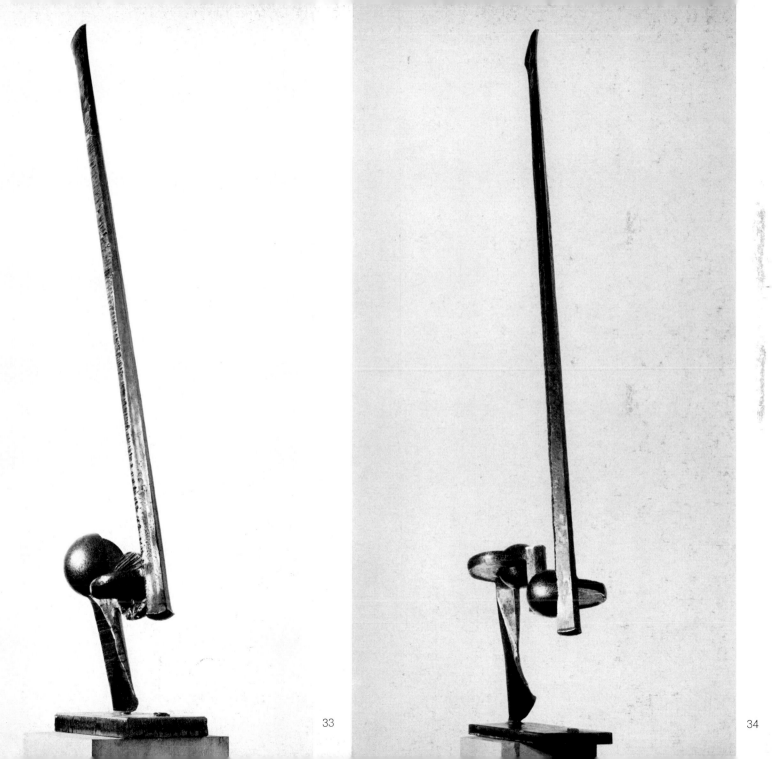

33

34

35

36

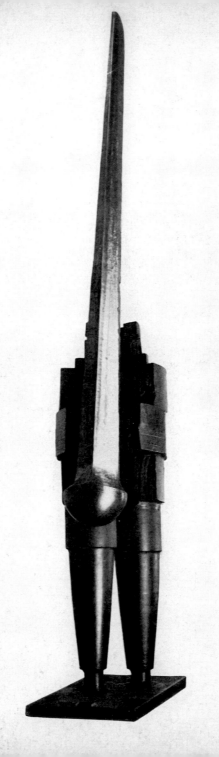

38

39

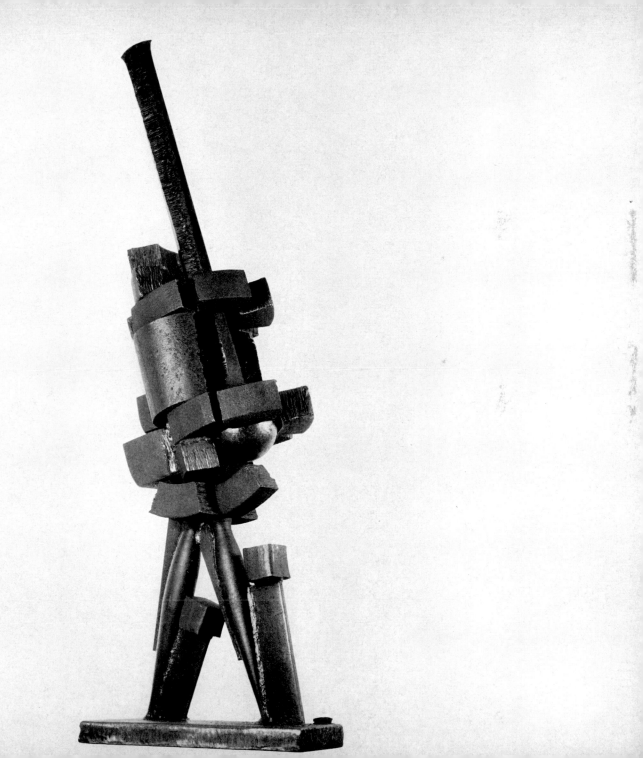

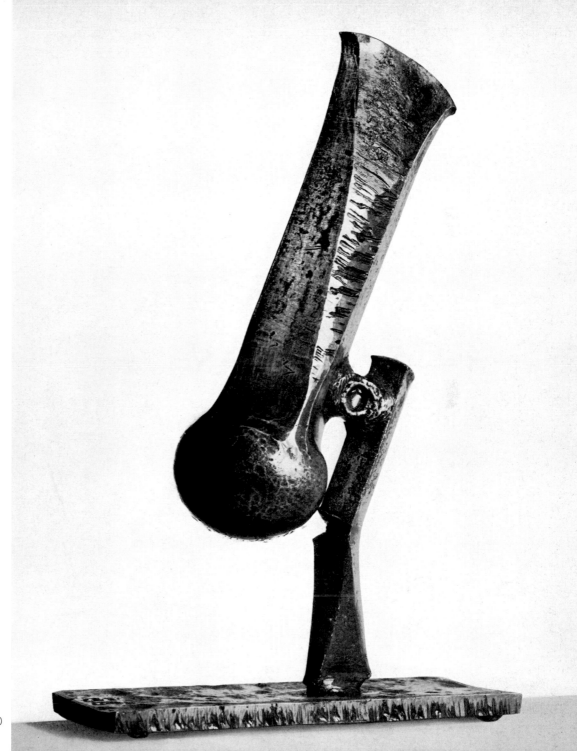

40

41

42

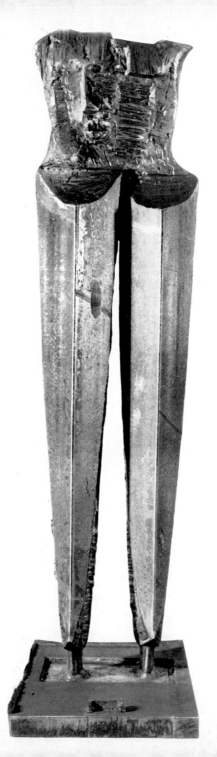

43

▷ 44, 45

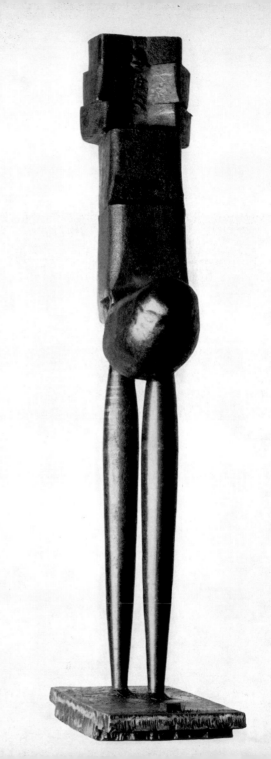

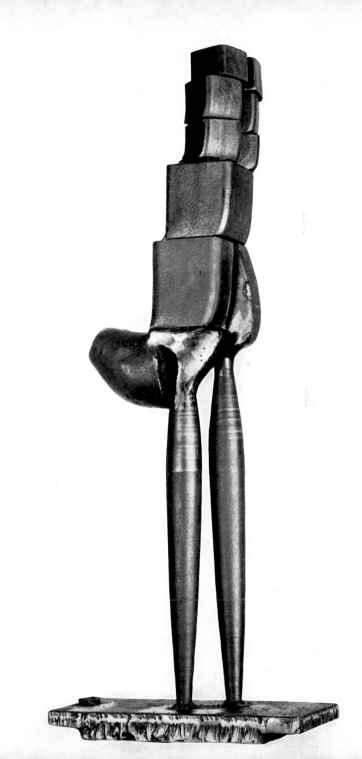

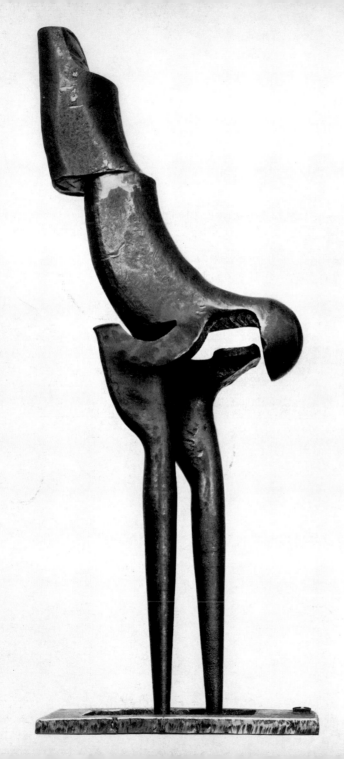

48

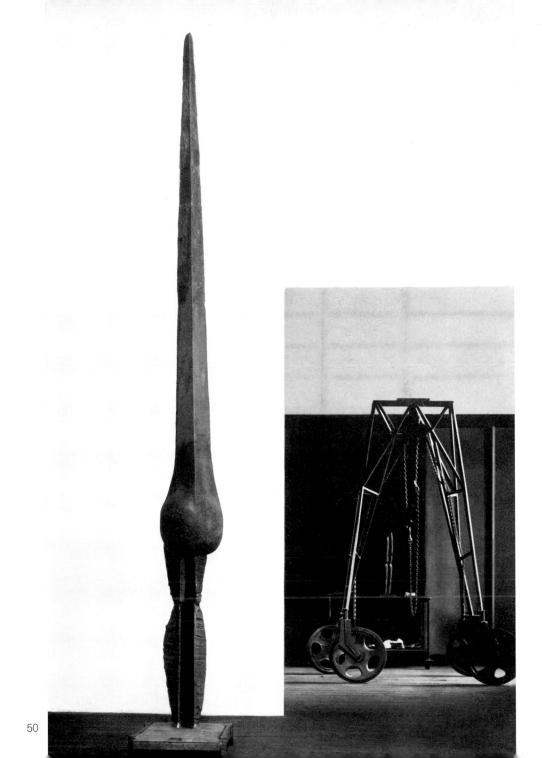

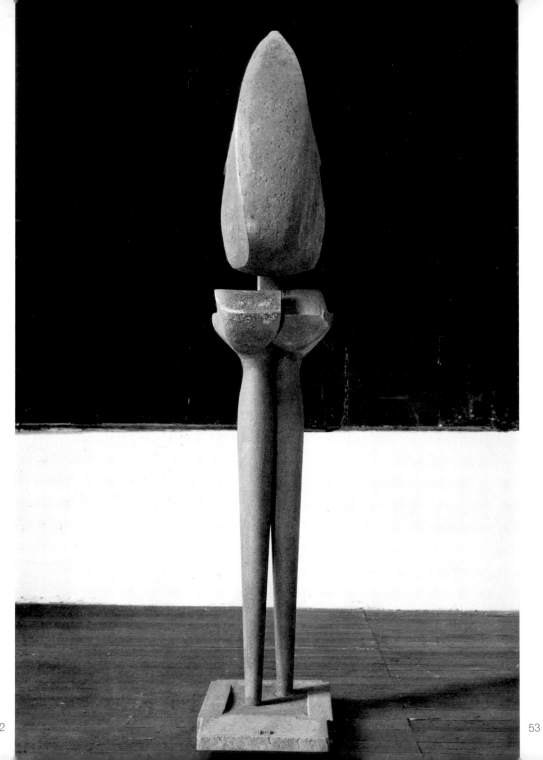

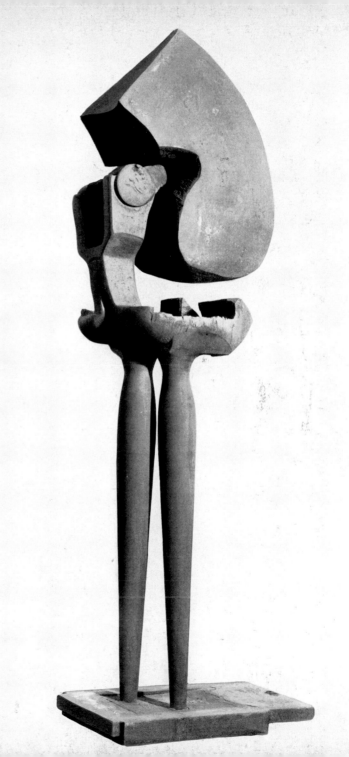

55

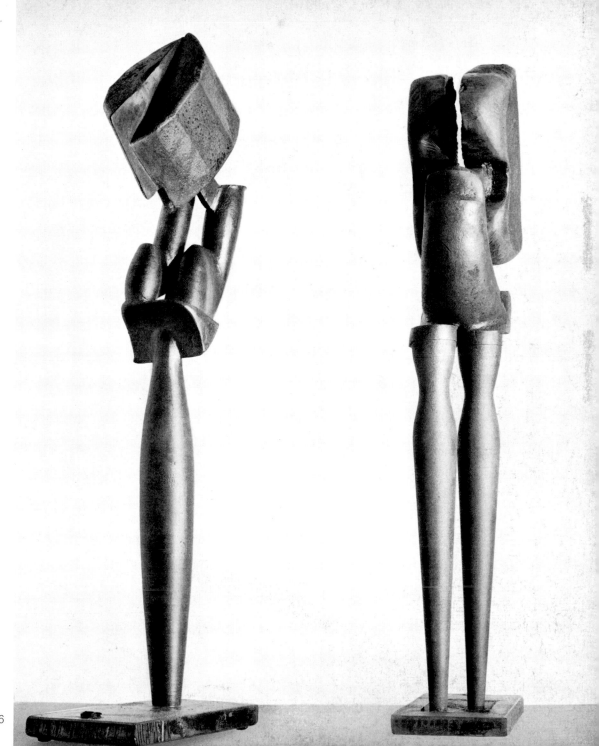

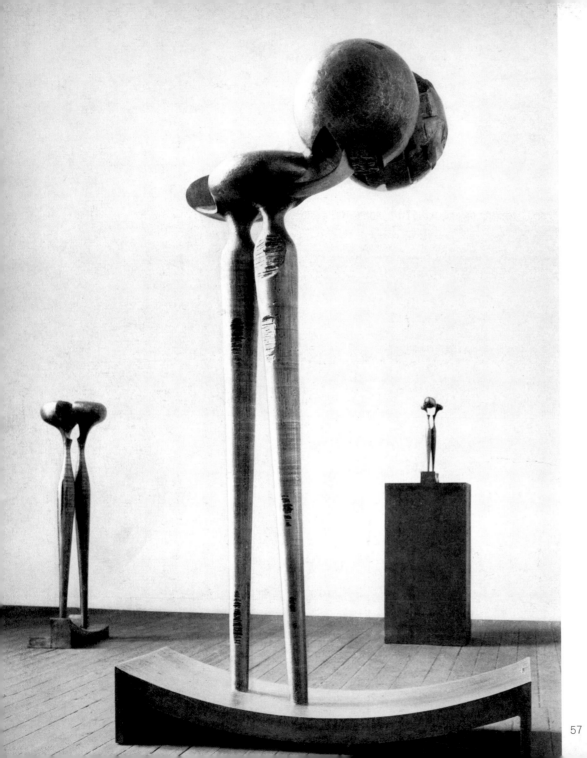

59

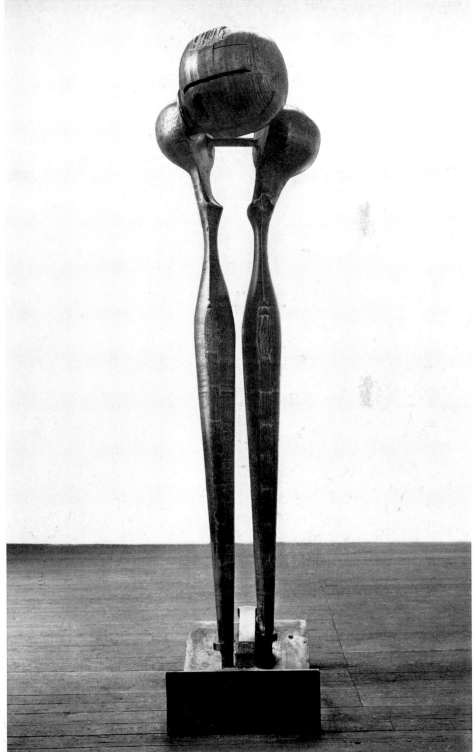

61

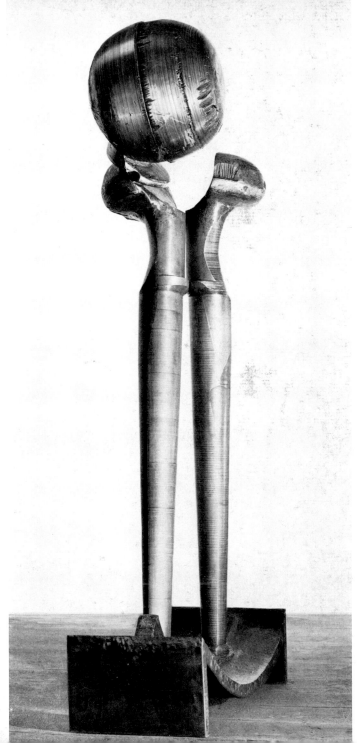

65

List of Plates

Measurements refer to height. All sculptures illustrated are of iron. When no owner-
ship is mentioned, the sculpture is in the artist's collection.

Biography

1916	Born in Linz
1932–1936	Attended State Technical School for Engineering, Linz
1936–1938	Studied architecture at the University of Graz
1938–1940	Studied at the Academy of Art, Vienna
1939–1945	Served in the war
1945–1951	Teacher at the Art School, Linz
1951	Moved to Vienna
1954	Grant from UNESCO—six months in Greece
1959	Awarded the City of Vienna Prize
1962	Called to the Academy of Art, Stuttgart

Exhibitions

One-Man Exhibitions

1951   Neue Galerie der Stadt Linz; Galerie d'Art moderne, Basle
1952   Galerie Würthle, Vienna
1960   XXXth Biennale at Venice
1963   Museum of the Twentieth Century, Vienna; Kunsthalle, Basle; Museum Folk-
       wang, Essen; Von der Heydt-Museum der Stadt Wuppertal; Württembergi-
       scher Kunstverein, Stuttgart
1964   Kunstverein, Hamburg; Stedelijk Museum, Amsterdam
1965   Odyssia Gallery, New York

Mixed Exhibitions

1953   II. Bienal do Museu de Arte Moderna de São Paulo
1954   XXVIIth Biennale at Venice
1956   XXVIIIth Biennale at Venice
1956/57 "Art from Austria": Stedelijk Museum, Amsterdam, Museum, Eindhoven,
       Kunsthalle, Bern, Kunsthalle, St. Gallen
1957   4th Biennale de la Sculpture, Antwerp, Middelheim Park
1958   World Exhibition at Brussels, Austrian Pavilion
1959   5th Biennale de la Sculpture, Antwerp, Middelheim Park; "Documenta II":
       Cassel
1960   "Austrian Painting and Sculpture, 1900–1960": London, The Arts Council o
       Great Britain
1961   2e Exposition internationale de la sculpture contemporaine: Musée Rodin,
       Paris; The Hanover Gallery, London, Summer Exhibition 1961; The Pittsburgh
       International Exhibition; Concorso internazionale del bronzetto, Padua; The
       Stanley Seeger Jr. Collection, Princeton University; The World House Gallery,
       New York
1962   Museum of the Twentieth Century, Vienna, Opening Exhibition; Gimpel &
       Hanover Gallery, Zurich, Opening Exhibition
1963   Concorso internazionale del bronzetto, Padua; "Idols and Demons": Museum
       of the Twentieth Century, Vienna
1964   "Masterpieces of Sculpture": Museum of the Twentieth Century, Vienna;
       Wilhelm-Lehmbruck-Museum, Duisburg, Opening Exhibition; "Documenta
       III": Cassel; "Decade 54–64": Tate Gallery, London; I. Internationale der Zeich-
       nung, Darmstadt; World Fair, New York, Austrian Pavilion
1965   Sculpture internationale, Amsterdam, Vondelpark